Fun Holiday Crafts
Kids Can Do!

St. Patrick's Day Crafts

Carol Gnojewski

Enslow Publishers, Inc.

40 Industrial Road   PO Box 38
Box 398   Aldershot
Berkeley Heights, NJ 07922   Hants GU12 6BP
USA   UK

http://www.enslow.com

Library of Congress Cataloging-in-Publication Data

Gnojewski, Carol.
   St. Patrick's Day crafts / Carol Gnojewski.
      p. cm.
   Summary: Provides information about the origin and customs of St. Patrick's Day, ideas for celebrating this holiday, and directions for making such crafts as an Irish shamrock, a Blarney Stone, Celtic jewelry, and Wee Ones puppets.
   Includes bibliographical references and index.
   ISBN 0-7660-2256-0 (hardcover)
   1. Saint Patrick's Day decorations—Juvenile literature.
2. Handicraft—Juvenile literature. [1. Saint Patrick's Day.
2. Handicraft. 3. Holidays.] I. Title: Saint Patrick's Day crafts.
II. Title.
TT900.S25G56 2004
745.594'166—dc21
                      2003010330

Printed in the United States of America

10 9 8 7 6 5 4 3

To Our Readers: We have done our best to make sure all Internet Addresses in this book were active and appropriate when we went to press. However, the author and the publisher have no control over and assume no liability for the material available on those Internet sites or on other Web sites they may link to. Any comments or suggestions can be sent by e-mail to comments@enslow.com or to the address on the back cover.

Illustration credits: Crafts prepared by June Ponte.
Photography by Carl Feryok.

Cover Illustration: Carl Feryok

Contents

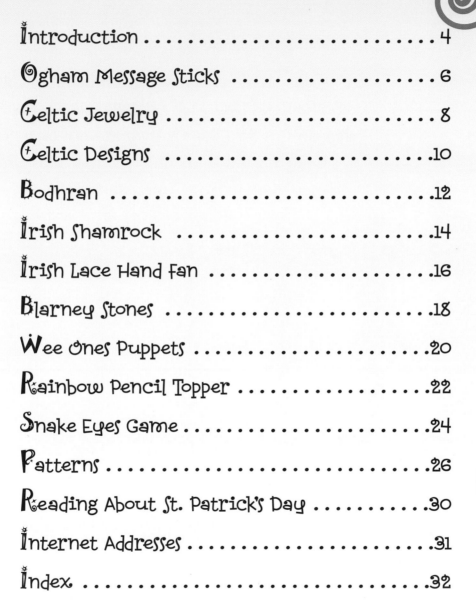

Safety Note: Be sure to ask for help from an adult, if needed, to complete these crafts!

Introduction

Each year on March 17, we celebrate Irish culture on St. Patrick's Day. Many people wear something green on this day, even if they are not Irish. They have parties and march in parades. Some may even look for leprechauns!

This holiday honors St. Patrick, the patron saint of Ireland. But he was not Irish. When St. Patrick was young, he lived with the Celtic (KEL-tik) people in Ireland as a slave. Later, he escaped. He returned to Ireland as a missionary for the Catholic Church.

St. Patrick's Day is a holy day in Ireland. Irish colonists first introduced the holiday to America in 1737. Although St. Patrick's Day is not a national holiday in the United States, many Americans celebrate it.

The crafts in this book will help you to celebrate St. Patrick's Day. Decorate your home with a festive shamrock or two. Play an Irish song on a bodhran. Leave secret holiday messages for your friends with an Ogham message stick. But most of all, remember that on St. Patrick's Day, everyone can enjoy the celebration— even if they are not Irish!

Ogham Message Sticks

St. Patrick met Irish people who spoke a Celtic language called Gaelic (GAY-lik). They used an alphabet called Ogham (ohm). It was made up of lines and dots.

What You Will Need:

- paint stirrers or large craft sticks
- green marker
- ruler (optional)
- lined paper
- pencil

1. Draw a line down the center of each paint stirrer or craft stick with the green marker. Use a ruler if needed.

2. Next, use a pencil to draw a line down the center of a piece of lined paper.

3. Write the letters of the alphabet in a column down the right-hand side of the paper.

4. Make a symbol for each alphabet letter. Use lines, dashes, and dots. Or, use symbols such as stars, moons, rings, waves, or flower shapes. This will be your Ogham code-breaker sheet.

5. Write secret messages to friends on the sticks. Don't forget to give them copies of your code-breaker sheet so they can decode your messages and send you some of their own!

Draw a green line
down the center . . .

make up your
secret code . . .

Send secret messages
to all your friends!

Holiday Hint:

For fun at a St. Patrick's Day party, put an Ogham message stick with a guest's name at every place setting. Put a copy of the code-breaker sheet on the the table. See who can find their seat first!

7

Celtic Jewelry

In St. Patrick's time, Irish people, or Celts (kelts), lived in tribal clans. Celts wore metal jewelry to show their importance in the clan. They wore jewelry on their fingers, wrists, ankles, and arms. Around their necks they wore metal collars or neck chains called torques (torks).

What You Will Need:

- aluminum foil
- ruler
- large pipe cleaners
- washers or nuts (optional)

1. Tear off a 4-inch length of aluminum foil. Starting at the bottom of the long end, roll it up tightly to make a foil snake.

2. Straighten the pipe cleaners and place the foil snake between them. The pipe cleaners should be a little longer than the foil.

3. Twist one pair of pipe cleaner ends together. Wrap the pipe cleaner ends back and forth to braid them around the foil. At the end of the foil, twist the remaining pipe cleaner ends together.

4. Bend the foil around your wrist, ankle, or upper arm. Twist the ends together.

5. To make a neck torque, follow directions 1–3. Then, cut a long pipe cleaner in half.

6. Thread one pipe cleaner half through a washer or nut and even out the ends. Twist twice to hold on the washer or nut.

7. Wrap the pipe cleaner ends around one end of the torque.

8. Repeat with another washer or nut and the second pipe cleaner half. The torque will have washers or nuts on both ends.

Start by rolling some aluminum foil . . .

Wrap pipe cleaners around the foil . . .

Add washers to the end of the torque . . .

Your Celtic jewelry is ready to wear!

Holiday Hint:

Celtic jewelry makes a great holiday gift. Make bracelets and torques for your friends and family to wear on St. Patrick's Day.

Celtic Designs

Irish monks copied books by hand. They decorated the pages with Celtic designs in gold and brightly colored inks. Celtic artists drew geometric shapes and used spirals and knots in their designs.

What You Will Need:

- scissors
- plastic food container lids
- hole punch
- masking tape roll
- unlined paper
- colored pens or pencils

1. Cut the plastic lids into large shapes such as circles, ovals, triangles, or squares.

2. Punch holes in the shapes in different places.

3. Set the roll of masking tape on the paper. It will be the border for your designs.

4. Place a plastic shape inside the tape roll.

5. Stick a colored pen or pencil into one of the holes in the shape.

6. Move the colored pen or pencil and the shape clockwise around inside the tape roll. As you move the shape, it should touch the inside of the tape roll.

7. Put the pen or pencil in a different hole in the same shape. Try another pen or pencil color as you move from hole to hole in each shape.

Carefully cut the lids into shapes. . .

Place one of the shapes inside the tape roll. . .

Use a pen to move the shape around. . .

Display your Celtic design for all your family and friends to see!

Holiday Hint:

Design a St. Patrick's Day card to give to a friend. Decorate the card with Celtic designs in bright, colorful patterns.

Bodhran

The bodhran (BOW-ron) is an Irish drum. It has a round wooden frame with an animal skin stretched over it. A bodhran is played with a two-sided wooden beater called a tipper. You can change the tone by pressing your hand against the back of the drum head as you play it.

What You Will Need:

- scissors
- paper bag
- embroidery hoop
- crayons or markers
- unsharpened pencil
- penciltop or regular erasers
- tape
- pipe cleaners (optional)

1. Cut a circle in the paper bag that is bigger than your embroidery hoop. This will be the "skin," or drumhead.

2. Decorate the center of the circle with crayons or markers. Make Celtic designs (such as the ones on pp. 26–28) or draw an Irish symbol, such as a shamrock or a harp.

3. Arrange the decorated circle on top of the inner embroidery hoop. Try to center it so that it is evenly spaced all around.

4. Attach the outer hoop. Then, tighten the tension knob to stretch the bag circle as tight as possible.

5. To make a tipper, put pencil top erasers on each side of the unsharpened pencil. If you only have regular erasers, tape them securely onto each side of the pencil. If you like, add some pipe cleaners for decoration.

Carefully cut the paper bag. . .

Decorate the circle. . .

Make the tipper for your bodhran. . .

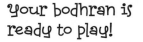

Your bodhran is ready to play!

Holiday Hint:

Use the tipper to beat rhythms on your bodhran. A light touch makes the best sound. Invite friends over on St. Patrick's Day to enjoy an afternoon of drumming—the Irish way!

Irish Shamrock

The shamrock is a green plant that grows in Ireland. It has three leaves. This Irish shamrock has three colors—green, white, and orange—the colors of the Irish flag.

What You Will Need:

- pencil
- green, white, and orange construction paper
- scissors
- brads
- markers

1. Draw a large heart shape on each color of construction paper. (If you like, use the pattern on page 29.) Cut out the hearts. These will be the three shamrock leaves.

2. Arrange the hearts so that their points face down. Place the white heart in the center. Put the green heart on the left and the orange heart on the right. The points of the green and orange hearts should overlap on top of the white heart.

3. Cut a stem from the green construction paper.

4. Poke a brad through the top of the stem and then through all three heart points.

5. Fasten the brad in the back of the white heart. Then, open up the hearts to form a shamrock. Decorate your shamrock with the markers.

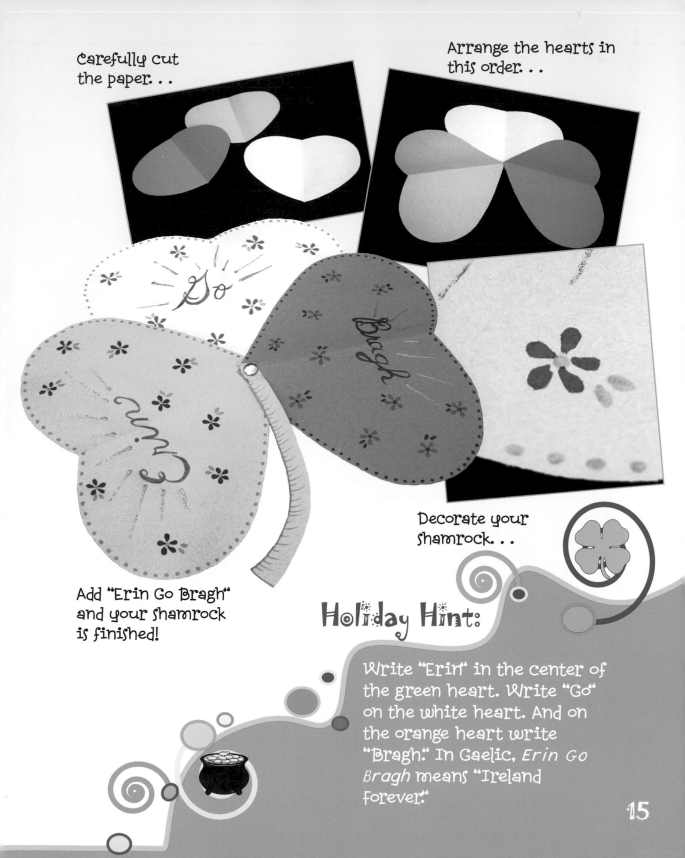

Carefully cut the paper. . .

Arrange the hearts in this order. . .

Go

Bragh

Erin

Add "Erin Go Bragh" and your shamrock is finished!

Decorate your shamrock. . .

Holiday Hint:

Write "Erin" in the center of the green heart. Write "Go" on the white heart. And on the orange heart write "Bragh." In Gaelic, *Erin Go Bragh* means "Ireland Forever."

15

Irish Lace Hand Fan

Lacemaking was often taught to Irish girls. They used fine thread to crochet delicate patterns. Some of the prettiest lace was used to make fans. Ladies carried these fans to parties and special events.

What You Will Need:

- white paper plate
- crayons or markers
- tissue paper
- scissors
- white glue
- hole punch
- thin ribbon or yarn
- tape
- lace scraps (optional)

1. Fold the paper plate in half so that the bottom faces out.

2. Flatten one or both sides. Decorate with crayons or markers.

3. Trace the folded plate on a piece of tissue paper. Cut out the half circle you traced.

4. Glue the half-circle onto one side of the decorated plate.

5. Hold the plate so that the fold faces down. The open end should be up. Punch holes through the half plate with the tissue paper, not both half plates.

6. Tape one end of a piece of ribbon or yarn to the inside of the half plate with holes.

7. Thread the ribbon or yarn through the holes. Then, tape the end of the ribbon or yarn to the inside of the plate or tie it so that the ends dangle decoratively downward.

8. Spread glue on the inside rim of both half plates and glue them together. If you like, glue some scraps of real lace inside so that just the edges show.

Fold a paper plate in half and punch holes around the edges. . .

Add the tissue paper and decorate it with green shamrocks. . .

Finish your fan with some ribbon and lace!

Holiday Hint:

Many people do traditional Irish dances, such as the reel, the jig, or the hornpipe, during St. Patrick's Day. You can use your fan to cool off after a spirited night of dancing!

Blarney Stones

Blarney (BLAHR-nee) means sweet talk or flattery. It is the ability to talk yourself into or out of anything. Some Irish people believe that to be able to do this, you must kiss the Blarney Stone in Ireland.

What You Will Need:

- flat, light-colored stones
- permanent markers or paint pens
- white glue
- bowl or paper cup
- water
- paintbrush
- glitter (optional)

1. Start with some clean, dry stones. Use markers or paint pens to write a word or words on each stone. Write something that reminds you of a person—words such as smart, kind, or helpful. Or write a wish for someone, like friendship, happiness, or good luck.

2. Squeeze glue into a bowl or paper cup. Slowly add water to make a thin glue "soup," stirring with the paintbrush. Use a mixture of three parts glue to one part water.

3. Paint the entire rock with the glue mixture to seal your message.

4. If you wish, sprinkle glitter on your blarney stones before the glue dries.

Wash and dry the stones. . .

Mix up some glue and water. . .

Friendship

Good Luck

Peace

Write a different message on each one and give to a friend!

Holiday Hint:

Exchange blarney stones with your friends or family members. A well-chosen word can make a meaningful gift for St. Patrick's Day!

Wee Ones Puppets

In Irish folktales, there are many kinds of magical creatures. Some make mischief and some grant wishes. St. Patrick's Day, features leprechauns—the "wee ones." People believed leprechauns were shoemaker elves only as big as your thumb.

What You Will Need:

- white glue
- bowl or paper cup
- water
- roll of toilet paper
- green tissue paper
- paintbrush
- fine-point marker
- cotton or Easter grass
- pipe cleaner (optional)

1. Squeeze some glue into the bowl or cup. Add one part water to three parts glue and mix well. The mixture should be like a thin glue soup.

2. Wrap a layer of toilet tissue around your thumb three or four times. Then, dip your wrapped thumb into the glue mixture. Be sure to cover all the toilet paper with glue. Mold the wet paper around your thumb.

3. Add another layer of toilet paper. Then, dip your thumb into the glue mixture again. Wrap, dip, and mold the paper around your thumb two or three more times. You need a thick, sturdy base.

4. Pointing the thumb down, gently unmold the paper thumb by sliding it off from the bottom. Let it dry overnight.

5. When the paper thumb is dry, put it on your thumb or another finger. Wrap green tissue paper around it. Use your finger or a paintbrush to coat the tissue paper with the glue mixture. Let it dry.

6. When it is dry, draw a face with a marker. Glue cotton or Easter grass to the top of the paper thumb for hair. If you like, glue a pipe cleaner to the bottom of the "neck" for a collar.

Mix up some glue. . .

Dip your wrapped thumb in the glue mixture and let it dry. . .

Add a face and some hair and your puppet is ready to perform!

Holiday Hint:

Wee ones make great decorations and finger puppets. Use your puppets in a play about the wee ones for your friends and family on St. Patrick's Day.

Rainbow Pencil Topper

This colorful rainbow will not lead you to leprechaun gold, but it will brighten your day!

What You Will Need:

- scissors
- Styrofoam® cup
- cotton swabs
- red, green, and blue paint
- hole punch
- unsharpened pencil

1. Carefully cut out the round bottom of a white Styrofoam cup.

2. Dip one end of a cotton swab in the red paint.

3. Use the swab to make red paint dots on the Styrofoam circle.

4. Do the same with the green and blue paints. The Styrofoam circle should be covered with red, green, and blue paint dots. Let the paint dry.

5. Punch a hole in the center of the Styrofoam circle.

6. Poke an unsharpened pencil through the hole. Place the Styrofoam circle near the eraser end of the pencil.

7. Spin the pencil between the palms of your hands. Look at the pencil topper as you spin the pencil. The red, green, and blue dots will blend together to make a rainbow.

Paint your styrofoam circle. . .

Get a couple of pencils. . .

Place the topper near the eraser and spin away!

Holiday Hint:

You can make more pencil toppers using the Styrofoam sides of the cup. Cut different shapes. Change the amount of red, green, and blue dots. See what new colors you can make as you spin the rainbow pencil toppers.

23

Snake Eyes Game

Did you know that there are no snakes in Ireland? Some stories say that St. Patrick drove away the snakes by beating on a drum. Others say he led them into the Irish Sea, where they drowned.

What You Will Need:

- markers
- shoe box or cardboard box
- scissors
- marbles

1. Draw a thick, coiled snake on the bottom of the box with markers.

2. Cut holes along the snake's body and where its eyes should be. For each hole, poke a blade of the scissors through from the inside of the box and twist. Make the holes just wide enough so that the marbles will rest on top, but not fall through.

3. Counting by threes, number each hole. Start at the tail and move toward the snake's eyes. The hole closest to the tail will be 3. The next hole will be 6. The one after that will be 9, and so on. The holes for the eyes should have the largest numbers.

4. Place the marbles inside the box. There should be two fewer marbles than there are holes.

5. Move the box from side to side until each marble rests in a hole.

6. Write down the number next to each marble. Add the numbers together. That is your score—the number of snakes you drove away!

Draw a snake in the shoe box. . .

Cut holes and number them. . .

Add the marbles. . .

See who can get the highest score!

Holiday Hint:

This is a fun game to play with a friend on St. Patrick's Day. See how many snakes you can drive away!

Patterns

Use tracing paper to copy the patterns on these pages. Ask an adult to help you cut and trace the shapes onto construction paper.

Use a copier to enlarge or shrink the design to the size you want.

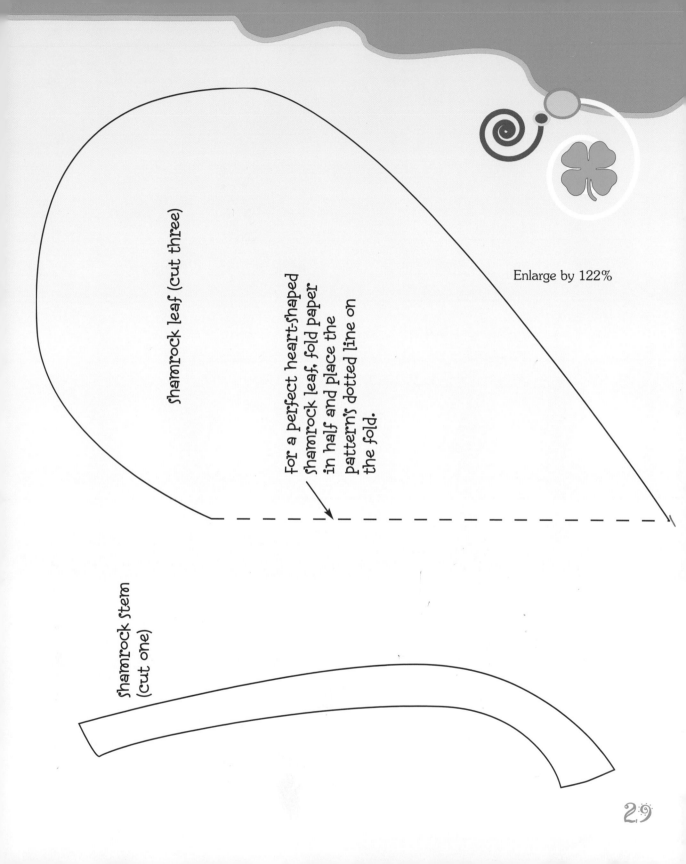

Shamrock leaf (cut three)

For a perfect heart-shaped shamrock leaf, fold paper in half and place the pattern's dotted line on the fold.

Enlarge by 122%

Shamrock stem (cut one)

Gibbons, Gail. *St. Patrick's Day*. New York: Holiday House, 1994.

Gillis, Jennifer Blizen. *St. Patrick's Day*. Chicago: Heinemann LIbrary, 2003.

Landau, Elaine. *St. Patrick's Day—Parades, Shamrocks, and Leprechauns*. Berkeley Heights, N.J.: Enslow Publishers, Inc., 2002.

Roop, Peter and Connie. *Let's Celebrate St. Patrick's Day*. Brookfield, Conn.: Millbrook Press, 2003.

Rosinsky, Natalie M. *St. Patrick's Day*. Minneapolis: Compass Point Books, 2003.

Ross, Kathy. *Crafts for St. Patrick's Day*. Brookfield, Conn.: Millbrook Press, 1999.

HistoryChannel.com: The History of St. Patrick's Day

Find out more about the holiday, St. Patrick, and famous Irish personalities.

<http://www.historychannel.com/exhibits/
stpatricksday/main.html>

Kids Domain: St. Patrick's Day

You can find online games, crafts, and clip art on this great Web site.

<http://www.kidsdomain.com/holiday/patrick/>

Index